Bedtime

Gill Tanner and Tim Wood

Photographs by Maggie Murray

Illustrations by Pat Tourret

A & C Black · London

Here are some of the people you will meet in this book.

The Hart family in 1990 **The Cook family in 1960**

Lee Hart is the same age as you.
His sister Kerry is eight years old.
What is Lee's mum called?

This is Lee's mum Linda when she
was just nine years old in 1960.
She is with her mum and dad,
her brother and her baby sister.

The Smith family in 1930

The Barker family in 1900

This is Lee's granny June,
when she was just a baby in 1930.
Her brother Jack is looking after her.

This is Lee's great grandma Lucy,
when she was six years old in 1900.
Can you see what her sister and her
brothers are called?

Can you spot the differences between these two photographs?
One shows bedtime in a modern house
and one shows bedtime one hundred years ago.

This book is about bedtime.
It will help you find out
how bedtime and going to bed
have changed in the last hundred years.

There are eleven mystery objects in this book
and you can find out what they are.
They will tell you a lot about people in the past.

These belonged to Charles and Alice Barker in 1900.
They wore them every night at bedtime.
Do you know what they are made of?
Can you guess what they are?

Turn the page to find out.

Charles and Alice are going to bed.
In those days, most people lived in small houses.
Young children, like Adam, slept in their parents' bedroom.
Can you spot the mystery objects in the picture?
They are Alice's **nightdress** and Charles' **nightshirt**.

In 1900, hardly anyone wore pyjamas.
Women and girls wore nightdresses.
Men and boys wore nightshirts.
Summer nightdresses and nightshirts were made of cotton.
Winter ones were made of flannel or thick cotton.
Do you have different nightwear for summer and winter?
What is it made from?

This mystery object was used
by the Barker children at bedtime.
The outside is made of blue glass.
It is about the same size as a mug.
Can you see what is inside the glass?
What do you think it is for?

Turn the page to find out.

Fred, Harry and Lucy are in bed listening to a story.
In those days, most children had to share
a bedroom with their brothers and sisters.
Fred and Harry slept in one bed.
Amy and Lucy slept in the other.
Can you see the mystery object? It's a **night light**.

In 1900, only a few homes had electric lights.
Amy read the bedtime story by candlelight.
When she finished she blew out the candle
but left the night light burning.
The night light kept the children company
and made them feel safe.
Do you have a night light?

This mystery object was put
in the children's beds at night.
It is about as long as your arm
from the elbow to the wrist.
It has a hole in the top and a stopper.
In winter, you may have something like this,
but it won't be made of pottery like this one.
Can you guess what it is?

Turn the page to find out.

Amy is getting ready for bed.
Can you see the mystery object in the picture?
It's a **stone hot water bottle**.

In 1900, most people used hot water bottles like this one to warm their beds.
The bottle wasn't really made of stone.
It was made of thick, heavy pottery.
Amy took her hot water bottle out of the bed before she went to sleep.
She did not like having the cold bottle in bed with her in the morning.

This mystery object is as long as your bed.
It belonged to May Smith in 1930.
She used it during the winter.
You may have something like it in your bedroom.
Do you know what is inside it?
What do you think it is called?

Turn the page to find the answers.

This is May Smith's bedroom in 1930.
How is it different from her mother's bedroom in 1900?
Can you spot the mystery object?
It's an **eiderdown**.
It is filled with feathers.

May and her mum are making May's bed.
In those days no one had duvets or fitted sheets.
The flat sheets and blankets had to be pulled tightly over the mattress and tucked in underneath.
In winter, Lucy put extra blankets and eiderdowns on the children's beds to keep them warm.

This belonged to Jack in 1930.
Do you have anything like it in your home?

Turn the page to find out what it is.

Jack is in bed reading his **book**.
In 1930, there were no televisions to watch.
The Smith family listened to the radio.
But there were no radio programmes
for children after 6 o'clock.

Jack read in bed every evening before he went to sleep.
His favourite book was 'Robin Hood'.
In those days, most books for children had hard covers,
like the book you are reading.
They didn't often have coloured pictures inside.
Do you have a favourite book?

These mystery objects were used by Lucy Smith in 1930.
They are about as long as your arm
from the elbow to the wrist.
One of the objects looks a bit like a long, thin candle.
A big clue is that they are all something to do with a fire.

Can you guess what they are?

Turn the page to find out.

Lucy is getting ready to feed baby June.
She is lighting the gas fire to warm the room.
Can you see the mystery objects?
They are **clays** and a **taper**.
The clays are in the gas fire.
The taper is in Lucy's hand.

In those days, hardly anyone had central heating.
Most houses were heated by coal, gas or electric fires.
Lucy used the taper to light the gas fire.
The gas flames heated the clays until they were red hot.
The clays helped to spread the heat into the room.

This belongs to Linda Cook in 1960.
Look carefully. It's not just a toy.
What do you think the zip is for?
Can you guess what it is?

Turn the page to find out.

This is Linda Cook's bedroom in 1960.
Does it look different from May Smith's
bedroom in 1930?
Linda's friend Cleo is staying the night.
Can you spot the mystery object?
It's a **nightdress case**.

The case is made of nylon
which was a new material in those days.
Linda's nightdress was also made of nylon.
Some people liked nylon because it was easy to wash
and did not need to be ironed.
Do you keep your nightclothes in a special case?

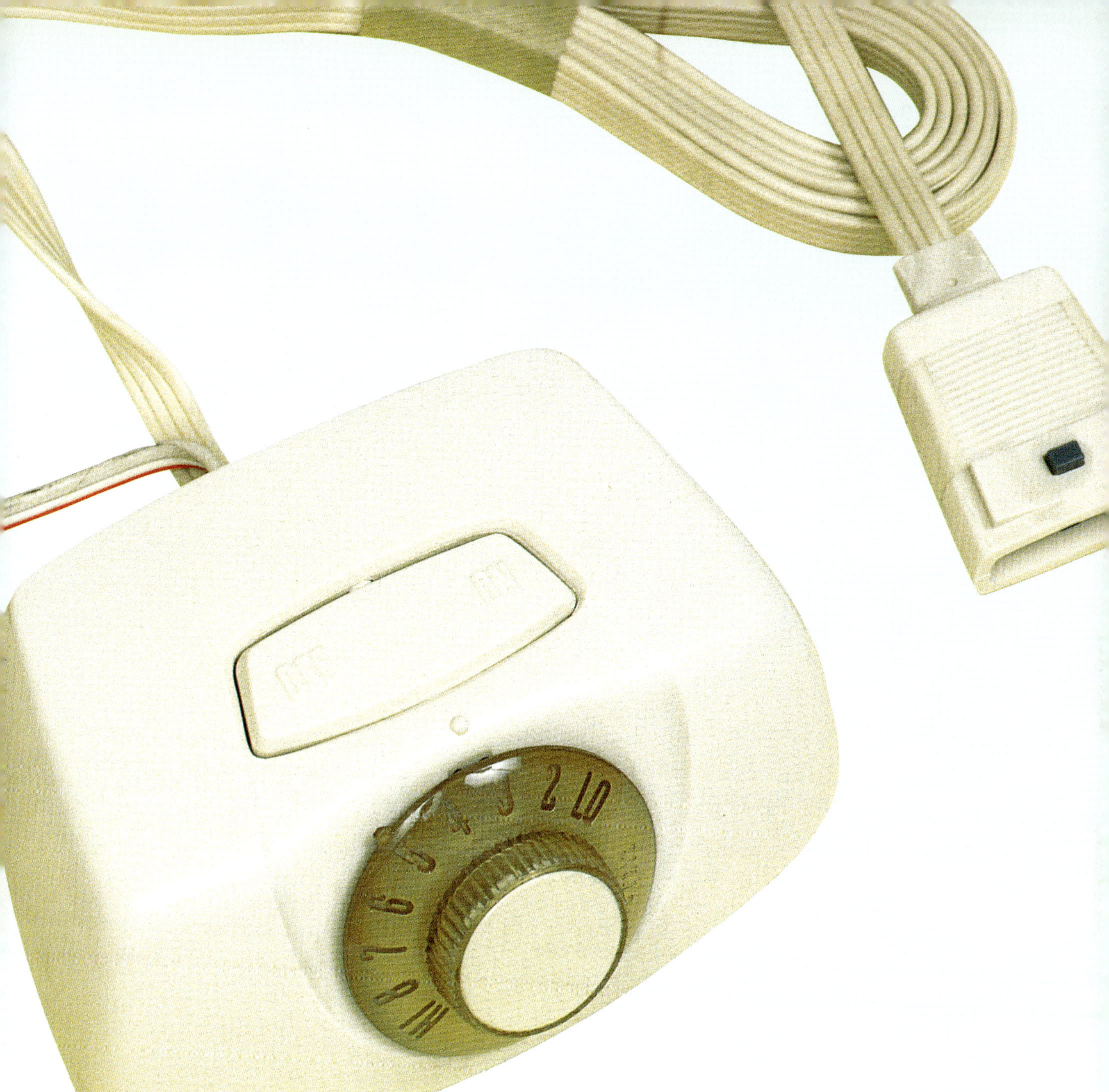

David and June Cook had one of these in their bedroom.
It is about the same size as it is shown here.
It works by electricity.
Can you guess why it has numbers on it?
What do you think it is?

Turn the page to find the answer.

David and June are going to bed.
Can you spot the mystery object in the picture?
It's an **electric blanket control**.

David or June used the control
to switch on the electric blanket
an hour before they went to bed.
They could make the blanket hotter or cooler
by turning the dial on the control.
By 1960, most houses had electricity.
Using an electric blanket
was a popular way of warming a bed.
Does anyone in your home have an electric blanket?

Now that you know a bit more about bedtime
and how it has changed over the last hundred years,
see if you can guess what this mystery object is.
It belonged to Alice Barker. It is made of china.
It kept something safe during the night.
Can you guess what?

You will find the answer on page 24.

Time-Line

These pages show you the objects in this book and the objects which we find in bedrooms nowadays.

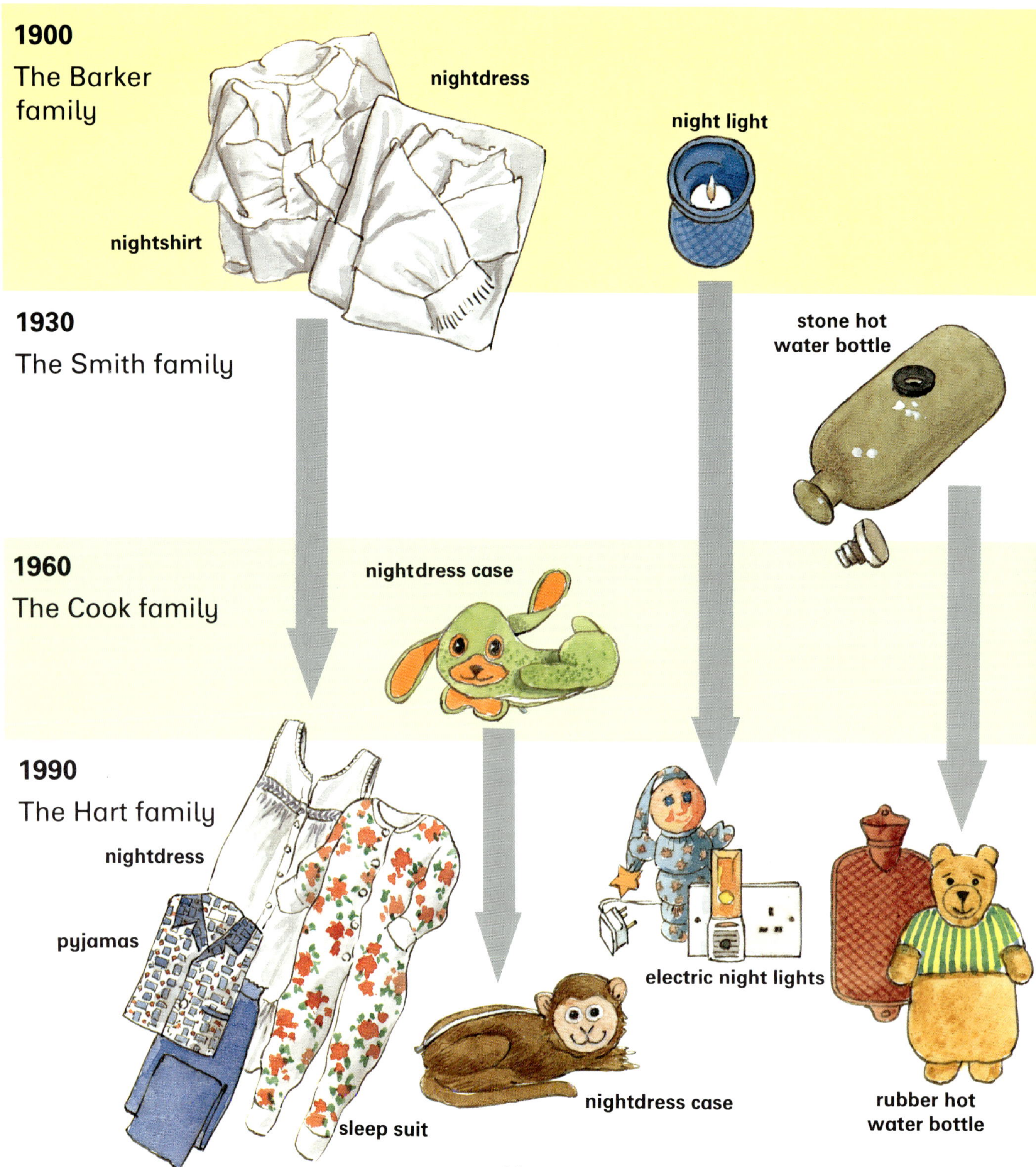

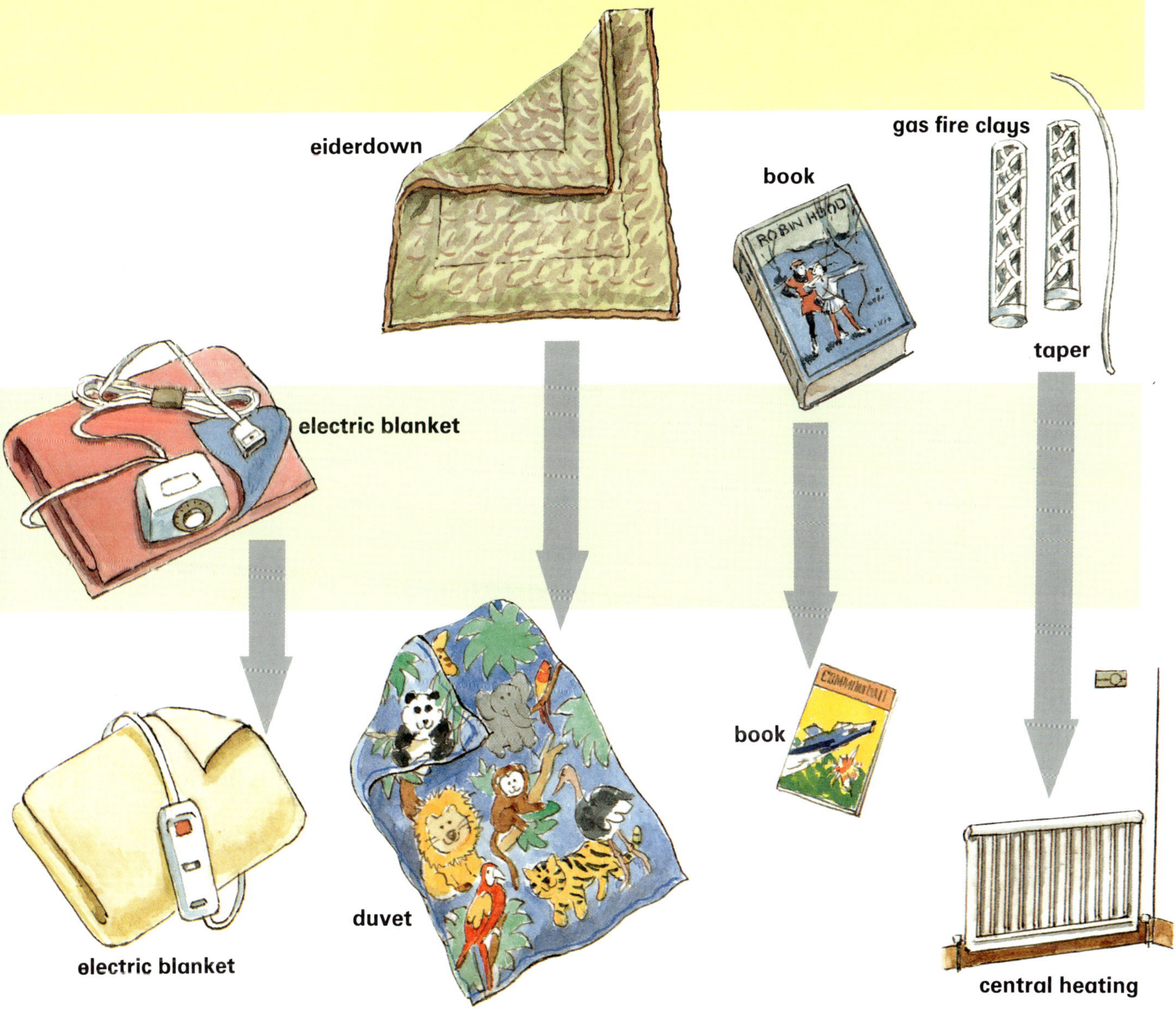
eiderdown
gas fire clays
book
taper
electric blanket
book
electric blanket
duvet
central heating

Index

The **mystery object** on page 21 is a china **ring holder**. Alice Barker used it every evening to keep her rings safe. She put the rings on the post which sticks up in the middle.

For parents and teachers

More about the objects and pictures in this book

Pages 5/6 The Barker family lived in a large industrial town. In 1900, all women wore nightdresses and all men wore nightshirts. Pyjamas came from India and became popular in the 1920s.

Pages 7/8 Night lights were slow-burning candles. They presented obvious dangers of fire. Electricity was not widely available until after 1926 when the National Grid was set up. By 1931, about 32% of households had electricity.

Pages 9/10 Stone hot water bottles were very heavy. The knob on the end made the bottle easier to carry. Poorer people used bricks heated in the range and wrapped in cloth to warm their beds.

Pages 11/12 The Smiths lived in a semi-detached house in a small town. Eiderdowns (so-called because of the eider duck feather filling) were used on top of layers of woollen blankets. Feather quilts remained popular on the continent and returned to Britain as duvets in the 1960s.

Pages 13/14 Paperback books were first produced in 1841. They did not become popular until 1935 with the publication of the first Penguin books. There were few colour illustrations in books in the 1930s.

Pages 15/16 The taper is like a long, thin candle. The clays radiated the heat of the flames and made the fire work more efficiently.

Pages 17/18 The Cooks lived in one of the new towns built in the 1960s. Nylon was invented in 1937. In the 1960s, nylon sheets and clothes became popular because they needed less care than cotton ones. Fluffy nylon material was used to make soft toys, such as the nightdress case.

Pages 19/20 Electric blankets were invented in 1927. Electrical household goods, such as electric blankets, started to become popular in the 1930s.

Things to do

History Mysteries will provide an excellent starting point for all kinds of history work. There are lots of general ideas which can be drawn out of the pictures, particularly in relation to the way beds, bedrooms, clothes, family size and lifestyles have changed in the last 100 years. Below are some starting points and ideas for follow up activities.

1 Work on families and family trees can be developed from the families on pages 2/3, bearing in mind that many children do not come from two-parent, nuclear families. Why do the families in the book have different surnames even though they are related? How have their clothes and hair styles changed over time?

2 Find out more about bedtime and bedrooms in the past from a variety of sources, including interviews with older people in the community, books and your local museum. Bedtime and bedrooms weren't the same for everyone. Why not?

3 There is one object which is in one picture of the 1900s, one picture of the 1930s, and one picture of the 1960s. Can you find it?

4 Make a local study collecting information about bedtime from older members of the community and/or arrange a field trip to a stately home or old house which has a bedroom or old bedroom furnishings on show.

5 Look at the differences between the photographs and the illustrations in this book. What different kinds of things can they tell you?

6 Make your own collection of bedtime and bedroom objects or pictures. You can build up an archive or school museum over several years by encouraging children to bring in old objects, collecting unwanted items from parents, collecting from junk shops and jumble sales. You may also be able to borrow handling collections from your local museum or library service.

7 Encouraging the children to look at the objects is a useful start, but they will get more out of this if you organise some practical activities which help to develop their powers of observation. These might include drawing the objects, describing an object to another child who must then pick out the object from the collection, or writing descriptions of the objects for labels or for catalogue cards.

8 Encourage the children to answer questions. What do the objects look and feel like? What are they made of? What makes them work? How old are they? How could you find out more about them? Do they do the job they are supposed to do?

9 What do the objects tell us about the people who used them? Children might do some writing, drawing or role play, imagining themselves as the owners of different objects.

10 Children might find a mystery object in their own home or school for the others to draw, write about and identify. Children can compare the objects in the book with objects in their own home or school.

11 If you have an exhibition, try pairing old objects with their nearest modern counterparts. Talk about each pair. Some useful questions might be: How can you tell which is older? Which objects have changed most over time? Why? What do you think of the older objects? What would people have thought of them when they were new? Can you test how well the objects work? Is the modern version better than the older version?

12 Make a time-line using your objects. You might find the time-line at the back of this book useful. You could include pictures in your time-line and other markers to help the children gain a sense of chronology. Use your time-line to bring out the elements of *change* (eg. the gradual development of better housing, smaller families, individual beds and bedrooms, central heating, electric blankets, fitted sheets and duvets) and *continuity* (eg. basic similarities in the need for sleep, warmth, beds, bedding and night clothes).

History Mysteries

First published 1993
A & C Black (Publishers) Limited
35 Bedford Row, London WC1R 4JH

ISBN 0-7136-3688-2

A CIP catalogue record for this book is available
from the British Library.

Acknowledgements

The authors and publishers would like to thank Mrs Tanner's Tangible History; Suella Postles and the staff of Brewhouse Yard Museum, Nottingham; Holly Prince; Madeline Moulton.

Photographs by Maggie Murray except for:
p4 (top) Gernsheim Collection, Harry Ransom Humanities Research Center, The University of Texas at Austin;
p4 (bottom) Ulrike Preuss, Format Photographers.

Filmset by Rowland Phototypesetting Limited, Bury St Edmunds, Suffolk
Printed and bound in Italy by L.E.G.O.